JUNIOR PET CARE

SNAKES

Photo: B. Kahl

ZUZA VRBOVA

Photography Susan C. Miller
Hugh Nicholas
With additional photos by Burkhard Kahl
Illustration Robert McAulay
Reading and Child Psychology Consultant
Dr. David Lewis

Snake Care Consultants
Chris Newman
Sue Paterson

ACKNOWLEDGMENTS

With special thanks to Len and Kim Simmons, Linton Zoo, and to
Chris Newman and Sue Paterson, Snake Care Specialists and
Directors of **Locusta**

Junior Pet Care

Guinea Pigs
Hamsters
Kittens
Parakeets
Puppies
Rabbits
Snakes
Turtles

This edition © 1998 Chelsea House Publishers, a division of Main Line Book Company.

1 3 5 7 9 8 6 4 2

Library of Congress Cataloging-in-Publication Data applied for

ISBN 0-7910-4910-8

CIP

CONTENTS

1 The Nature of a Snake   *page* **6**

2 Choosing a Snake   *page* **12**

3 A Home for Your Snake   *page* **20**

4 Feeding Your Snake   *page* **32**

5 Care for Your Snake   *page* **40**

Health Care for Your Snake   *page* **46**

Glossary   *page* **48**

NOTE TO PARENTS

Snakes have always been fascinating to us all—partly because they are so unlike us and other furry, cuddly mammals—like cats and dogs—who are often kept as pets. But snakes are easy and fun to keep. All they require is a small cage or tank, a light bulb, food and a little care. They are clean pets and most only need to be fed once or twice a week. They are quiet and beautiful and they all have their individual characters—just as we do. This book has been specially written for children of age 7 and upwards. It explains a snake's senses and ways in the wild, making it possible for a young child that is enthusiatic about snakes to have a happy and interesting pet.

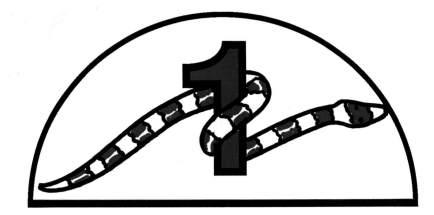

THE NATURE
OF A
SNAKE

Snakes belong to a group of animals called reptiles. Turtles and crocodiles and lizards are also reptiles. Dinosaurs were reptiles too. People often think of snakes as being cold and slimy creatures. But snakes are not unpleasant to touch. They have tough, scaly and nearly waterproof skins. The scales are clean and dry and can feel either rough or smooth.

All snakes are cylinder-shaped, but their fully-grown length varies a lot. The shortest snakes may only be as long as an adult's hand, while others, for example an anaconda or a python, may grow to be as long as a bus. These are some of the biggest living reptiles. There are many beautiful snakes found all over the world. They live in almost every country. Almost the only countries that do not have snakes are Ireland and New Zealand.

Snakes are often called *cold-blooded*. This is because the temperature inside their body is roughly the same as that of their surroundings. As snakes rely on the heat from the sun to warm their bodies, most snakes live in the warmer parts of the world. Those that live in cooler countries, such as parts of Europe and North America, *hibernate* during the winter. This means that they go into a very deep sleep and stay still in a sheltered place until warmer weather comes in spring.

Some species of snake are quite common although others are becoming rare. Snakes are not often seen in the wild because of their secretive habits. A good way of finding out and learning about snakes is to keep one as a pet.

Snakes are fascinating creatures. As some snakes can be dangerous because of their poison fangs, it is best to buy your snake from a pet store rather than trying to catch one from the wild.

Even if your snake was born in captivity, it is still a naturally wild animal and must be looked after properly. Many snakes need special care—keeping any animal is a responsible job. If your pet is healthy, happy and properly fed, you can learn a lot about snakes, just by watching their habits, general behavior and lifestyle.

Relaxing with a black King Snake (*Lampropeltis getulus nigritus*). Kingsnakes can eat other snakes, which is why their common name is Kingsnake.

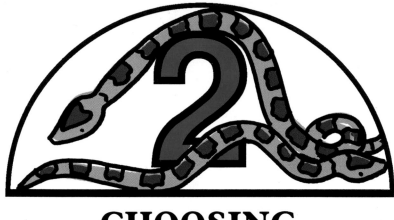

CHOOSING
A
SNAKE

It is important to buy a harmless snake. Some snakes use poison to kill their prey. Other snakes are constrictors, which coil themselves around their victims to kill them. A few very dangerous poisonous snakes do kill people, but most snakes are not harmful to people and there is no need to fear them.

Even dangerous snakes are interesting animals that bring benefits as well as harm. In some places snakes keep down the number of pests, like rats, for example. Also, scientists are learning more about human nerves and blood by studying the poison that snakes produce. Snake poison is called **venom.**

A good kind of snake for a beginner is a garter snake. It is easy to tame and feed and it adjusts well to changes in temperature and conditions. Other good snakes for beginners are corn snakes and kingsnakes. They are all beautiful to look at and come in many different color combinations.

A black Indigo (_Drymarchon corais couperi_) Snake from Florida is beautiful and gentle.

A Garter Snake (*Thamophis sirtalis*) is thin, which is why it is named after a garter.

The Sinaloan Milk Snake from Mexico (*Lampropeltis triangulum sinaloae*) does not feed on milk, but it does like mice.

The Royal Python (*Python regius*) is a good snake for a beginner.

A Royal Python
and a week old
baby Royal
Python. They
like mice and
are also known
as Ball Pythons.

An Eastern
Hognose
Snake
(*Heterodon
platyrhinos*).

The Leopard
Rat Snake
(*Elaphe
bimaculatus*) is
an ideal snake
for a young
beginner. It can
be tamed easily
and eats small
mice.

The Speckled
Kingsnake
(both views at
right) can be
very gentle, but
some are
vicious.

TAKING A SNAKE HOME

The best way of taking your snake home is to put it in a cloth bag or a pillow case. Make a knot in the bag at the top so there is no way your snake can escape. The cloth allows fresh air to circulate so the snake can breathe.

**Many people
are surprised to
discover that
snakes feel
dry, not slimy.**

When you buy your snake it is a
good idea to have a close look at it to
make sure it is fit and healthy, with
no cuts or grazes on its body. Also,
ask the owner what the snake is used
to eating.

A HOME
FOR
YOUR SNAKE

A home for a snake is called a vivarium (vy-vare-ee-um). It is simply an escape-proof box with a glass front and a tight-fitting lid. Snakes are very good at finding a weak corner of their cage, and it is amazing how small a crack a snake can squeeze through. Some people are frightened of snakes; coming across an escaped snake could be unpleasant for a friend or for another member of your family.

Once a snake has escaped, it can move surprisingly fast. Loose in a room, a snake can hide beneath the floorboards or in a nook or cranny so that you will not be able to find it or capture it again.

You can either buy a specially designed vivarium with glass sliding doors at the front (right) or you can buy an aquarium with a specially fitted lid which has a breathing vent and a built-in light fitting.

An all glass tank (below).

MAKING A VIVARIUM

An adult can help you make a comfortable vivarium for your pet. Alternatively, you can buy a ready-made one from your pet store.

A good vivarium can be made out of chipboard, laminated with a smooth plastic surface called **melamine.** Shelving boards made out of this kind of material are ideal. The joints between the panels can be sealed with a special aquarium sealant, available from some pet stores. Sealing the joints will help to stop dirt and insects collecting in the cracks. This kind of enclosure can be washed easily too.

The door can be made out of hinged flaps positioned in the top side of the unit. Additionally, you can have sliding doors to the front.

Warmth for your snake

It is important to make sure that your snake is warm enough. If snakes become cold they lose their appetite and they are more likely to catch an illness. As a guide they need to be kept at a temperature between 75 to 80°F.

You can buy from pet stores special vivarium heaters. The heaters give off enough warmth to keep your snake happy and healthy.

In the wild a snake will find shade from the sun—under a rock for example, if it becomes too hot. Or, if it is cold, it will find a warm spot where the ground has been heated by the sun's rays.

A vivarium heater. It is a specially-made mat—a bit like an electric blanket for a snake. You can put it below, above, behind or in your vivarium so it will not show.

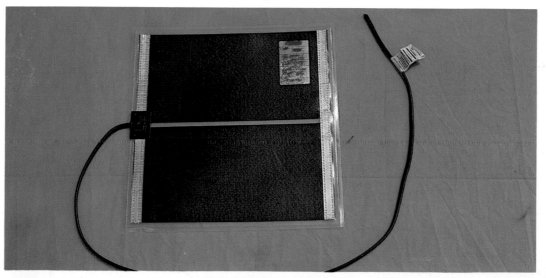

Although snakes often come from hot areas, they can also be killed if the temperature is too high.

Lighting in the vivarium

Light is also important for snakes. Natural sunlight is best because it stimulates snakes to produce **vitamin D3.** A snake cannot make this essential vitamin by just lying under a regular light bulb. The rays from the sun that help produce vitamin D3 are called ultraviolet rays and unfortunately these are filtered out by glass and plastic. But, you can buy special spectrum lights from pet stores so that your snake does not suffer from a vitamin deficiency.

A ceramic heater and fluorescent bulb provide heat and light in this snake cage, which is furnished simply and sensibly. A box for the snake to hide in is included in the setup.

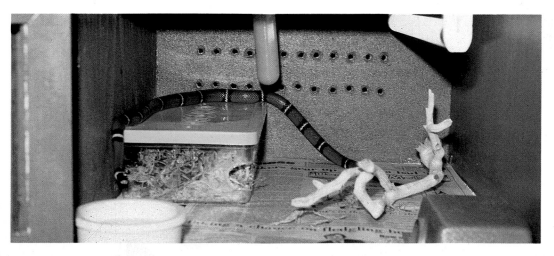

Making your snake at home

You will need to cover the floor of your vivarium with something that can be kept clean easily. It is best not to use any kind of sand as a floor covering as this will stick to your snake's food and your snake might swallow some of the sand by accident.

Coarse gravel is a safe floor covering and helps to make the vivarium an attractive feature of the room. You can just line the floor with newspaper

Bark chips made from Redwood tree bark which does not easily rot and is good in humid places. Bark looks good in a vivarium.

although this does not make the vivarium look very appealing. Another alternative is the processed corn cob bedding available in many pet shops.

Soil is not a sensible bedding material because tiny insects and bacteria might flourish in it and these might be harmful for your snake. Wood shavings are also not a good idea, because they might damage your snake's eyes.

Moss is pleasantly aromatic and very useful as a decorative material.

Decorating your vivarium

Most snakes are shy creatures and need to have places to hide. Pieces of cork bark provide good hiding places and make the vivarium look more interesting and attractive too. Try to plan your vivarium to look as similar to your snake's natural habitat as possible.

You can put some large stones or pebbles in the vivarium for your snake to bask in the heat on, or to hide behind. The rockwork may become stained by your snake's whitish droppings and so you should sometimes give the stones a wash.

Some snakes do not seem to drink very much but water will keep the vivarium moist and this helps to keep your snake in good condition.

Always provide a bowl of water in the vivarium.

When you decorate the vivarium you must make sure it is a safe place for your snake to be in. For example, never balance rocks on top of one another, otherwise they might fall on your snake and hurt it.

Plants always enhance a vivarium and create a natural look for your snake. You can simply put traditional house plants into the vivarium. The high humidity of a terrarium kills off most plants, so one should keep 2 sets of potted plants and alternate them every week or two. Leave the plants in their pots, buried in the floor covering, and remember to water them and remove any dead leaves. Do not use cacti, which with their sharp spines, could injure your snake.

Plastic plants are robust and with bark create an appealing setting.

Where to put a vivarium

Although plants and snakes enjoy some sunlight, you must make sure that you do not put the vivarium in direct sunshine. If you do this, the temperature inside can rise very rapidly and could kill your snake.

You will need to keep the vivarium very clean and so it is best to put it in a place that you can easily reach. You will need to wash the food dishes between meals and change the water pot every day.

A built-in vivarium.

SETTING UP A VIVARIUM

Cover the floor with a floor covering and put the water bowl in.

First put the heater in to keep your snake warm.

Finally, put your snake into his comfortable home.

FEEDING
YOUR
SNAKE

To understand your snake you must be aware of its senses. A snake cannot hear very well. You might have noticed that it has no ears. Instead the lower jaw can detect vibrations in the ground. Snakes do not have eyelids either.

Your snake's senses

Look carefully and you will see that they can never close their eyes. Each eye is protected by a transparent covering. Snakes generally have good eyesight.

The tongue plays an important part in a snake's senses. It is very sensitive to chemicals. The forked tongue can gather minute traces of chemicals from the ground or air so that the snake can taste or smell a scent trail.

Some snakes can also sense the body heat of their prey through heat sensors in their heads. You can see the heat receptors, called **pits** on some snakes, midway between the nostrils and the eyes in some poisonous snakes and on the lip scales of some boas. The pits allow snakes to find and strike at prey, even in the dark.

Eye with eye cap

Heat sensing pits

Forked tongue

Some snakes can sense the body heat of their prey through special heat sensors or "pits" in their heads.

How snakes eat

Most snakes have sharp backward pointing teeth, which they only use for grabbing and holding prey—rather than for chewing. A constricting snake grabs at its prey and then coils its body around the victim. Each time the victim breathes out, the snake tightens its grip. Eventually the creature suffocates and the snake will swallow it whole, head first.

Poisonous snakes have hollow fangs in their top jaw. Cobras have fixed front fangs and vipers have

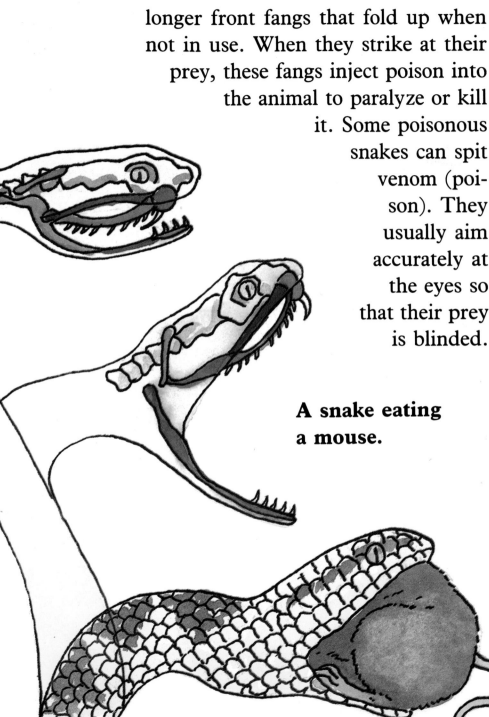

longer front fangs that fold up when not in use. When they strike at their prey, these fangs inject poison into the animal to paralyze or kill it. Some poisonous snakes can spit venom (poison). They usually aim accurately at the eyes so that their prey is blinded.

A snake eating a mouse.

What snakes eat

All snakes are predators and feed on other creatures. They are not vegetarians. Normally, in the wild they eat food that they kill themselves.

Most pet snakes like to feed on mice, rats or day-old chicks. Some people feel that snakes prefer their food to be offered live. But, this can be dangerous for your snake. Both rats and mice may bite and cause serious injuries to your snake with their sharp teeth. It is also not acceptable to many people to place such animals with your snake if they are alive. Instead, you should buy dead, frozen foods from pet suppliers.

One day old mice are a small snake's favorite food.

It is a good idea to make enquiries about a local source of snake food when you buy your snake. You will need to defrost any frozen animals you offer your snake very carefully, to make sure that there are no ice crystals in the food before you use it. Smaller snakes like to eat day-old mice, called **pinkies.**

If your snake is not used to eating dead food, move the mouse about on a feeding stick, a short distance away, to encourage it to strike out at the food. A snake's good sense of smell is

Elaphe longissima, **one of the rat snakes, is mainly a rodent eater. This species is aggressive.**

A Western Hognose eating a day-old mouse. You can see the bulge in the snake's body once the mouse has been swallowed.

very important in connection with its food. If your snake is refusing to eat, you can put an appetizing scent on the food to encourage it. You can persuade young garter snakes to eat fish by mixing it with earthworms, which they feed on when they have first hatched.

By offering the whole animal to a snake, the snake will have a complete and naturally balanced diet, with all the minerals and vitamins he needs. The food may be visible as a swelling inside the snake's body for several days. Gradually the snake's digestive juices dissolve it away.

Feeding requirements

Snakes have very efficient digestive systems and so they only need feeding once or twice a week. If your snake is lazy, has a tendency to be inactive, and stays in one place all the time, it might become fat and unhealthy.

CARE
FOR
YOUR SNAKE

Always approach a snake from above, never from its own level, and make sure your movements are slow and deliberate, rather than quick and jerky. Snakes, like all other reptiles, are likely to resent being handled if they are not used to it.

HANDLING YOUR
SNAKE SAFELY

The first few times you handle your snake, hold it with one hand around the neck—just at the back of the jaws so that it cannot turn and bite—and use the other hand to restrain the body. After a while, the snake will realize that it is not going to be hurt when it is being handled and will struggle less and less. The body of a snake is very sensitive and so you should never grip it tightly as you might bruise or injure your snake.

Hibernation

Many snakes, especially those that come from the colder parts of the world, hibernate during the winter. Just before hibernation, your snake will become more inactive and refuse to eat. If it is a healthy snake, it may not eat for several months. When the spring comes, your snake will become active and soon start accepting food again. In general, pet snakes kept indoors and warm do not need to hibernate and should not be forced to.

Kingsnakes like the one shown here are North American species that tend to hibernate.

The snake that shed this skin was very large.

Shedding the skin

From time to time, usually during the summer, snakes shed their skins to allow more room for them to grow. This is called **sloughing** (sluf-fing). The first slough takes place shortly after the creature has hatched. Then it occurs regularly throughout the animal's life.

For a few days before shedding the skin, the snake will become listless, its overall color becomes dull and a bluish-white film appears over the eyes. The snake begins shedding its

skin by rubbing its chin against a rough rock or a sharp branch until the outer skin splits and loosens around the head area. Then the snake literally crawls out of the skin, turning the skin inside out as it does so.

The skin is left behind in one piece and looks just like an empty snake. In captivity some snakes may have trouble in shedding their skin and may need some help. If your snake is overdue to shed, the skin will become dry, crackled and wrinkled.

You can buy vitamin drops to put in your snake's water bowl to keep your snake healthy.

HEALTH CARE FOR YOUR SNAKE

Snakes are usually healthy animals. People tend to worry if a snake does not feed, but healthy pet snakes have been known not to accept any food for periods as long as one year (although such long periods of non-feeding are to be avoided if at all possible). Small snakes must feed more often than large ones. It just seems strange to us that snakes only eat once a week or even once a month and can go for such long periods without food.

But, in captivity, snakes can catch diseases more easily than in the wild. Outdoors in their natural habitat snakes can change where they live and their diet easily, to get rid of mites, for example. If you feel that your snake may be unwell, it is wise to take it to a veterinarian.

Snake colds

One of the most common ailments of pet snakes is respiratory infections. This is usually due to the cage being kept too cool. The symptoms of a respiratory infection are wheezing and runny, wet nostrils and irregular, deep breathing. The condition can be treated by keeping the vivarium a little warmer and adding some vitamin supplements to your snake's food. You should also ask your veterinarian to treat your snake.

Mouth rot

This is one of the more serious diseases that sometimes infects snakes. It is caused by bacteria that kill the muscle and bone around the snake's mouth. Snakes that have this disease have creamy textured white patches in their mouths. Sometimes the teeth have been eaten away and the mouth has a bad smell. Mouth rot is hard to cure and it is a disease that other snakes can catch. If you think that your snake might have mouth rot, you should make sure that he is kept apart from other snakes. Take him to a veterinarian, who will probably prescribe a solution of mouthwash. This can be applied to the snake's mouth.

Mites

These can be a problem for snakes that live in captivity. Mites are black and only about the size of a pinhead. But, if you look carefully you can see them mostly around the snake's eyes and under his belly scales. The mites live on the snake's blood, which they suck. If you have more than one snake, the mites can easily spread to the rest of your collection. The treatment of mites must be thorough as mites can reinfect a snake. Pet shops sell preparations to kill mites.

The cage must be completely disinfected and all the gravel, bark, etc. replaced.

Glossary

Cold-blooded Snakes are cold-blooded because the temperature inside their bodies is nearly the same as the temperature of the outside air.

Constrictors Snakes that coil themselves around their victims and squeeze each time the animal breathes out, eventually strangling the prey.

Hibernate Snakes that live in colder areas of the world and cannot depend on the climate to keep their bodies warm will go into a deep sleep for the cold winter months.

Melamine A plastic covering, or lamination, used in the making of a vivarium.

Pinkies Another name for day-old mice, which are a favorite food of smaller snakes.

Pit Located midway between the nostrils and the eyes of a snake, the pits are heat receptors which help the snake find and aim at its prey.

Sloughing The process of shedding the snake's skin so that it will have room to grow.

Venom A poison made by snakes to kill their prey.

Vitamin D A necessary nutrient for snakes, available only through the sun's natural ultra-violet rays. Special spectrum lights, available at the local pet store, are an acceptable substitute.

Vivarium An escape-proof box for a pet snake to live in.

Index

cold-blooded, 8
Eastern Hognose
    Snakes, 16
feeding, 32
    pinkies, 37
    requirements, 39
Garter Snakes, 14
gravel, 26
handling, 42
health care, 46
    colds, 46
    mouth rot, 47

mites, 47
hibernation, 8, 43
Indigo Snakes, 14
Kingsnakes, 11
Leopard Rat Snakes, 17
Milk Snakes, 15
nature, 6
reptiles, 6
Royal Pythons, 15
selection, 12
senses, 33
shape, 7

shedding (sloughing),
    44
soil, 27
venom, 14
vitamin D3, 25
vivariums, 20
    building, 23
    decorating, 28
    lighting, 25
    location, 30
    melamine, 23
    temperature, 24